Sentence Models for Creative Writing

STUDENT BOOK

Chris Youles

hachette LEARNING

hachette LEARNING

Together we unlock every learner's unique potential

At Hachette Learning (formerly Hodder Education), there's one thing we're certain about. No two students learn the same way. That's why our approach to teaching begins by recognising the needs of individuals first.

Our mission is to allow every learner to fulfil their unique potential by empowering those who teach them. From our expert teaching and learning resources to our digital educational tools that make learning easier and more accessible for all, we provide solutions designed to maximise the impact of learning for every teacher, parent and student.

Aligned to our parent company, Hachette Livre, founded in 1826, we pride ourselves on being a learning solutions provider with a global footprint.

www.hachettelearning.com

To order, please visit www.HachetteLearning.com or contact Customer Service at education@hachette.co.uk / +44 (0)1235 827827.

ISBN: 978 1 0360 1987 7

First published in 2026 by
Hachette Learning (a trading division of Hodder & Stoughton Limited),
An Hachette UK Company
Carmelite House
50 Victoria Embankment
London EC4Y 0DZ

www.HachetteLearning.com

The authorised representative in the EEA is Hachette Ireland, 8 Castlecourt Centre, Dublin 15, D15 XTP3, Ireland (email: info@hbgi.ie)

Impression number 10 9 8 7 6 5 4 3 2 1
Year 2030 2029 2028 2027 2026

Illustrations by DC Graphic Design Limited, Hextable, Kent.
Typeset in the UK.
Printed and bound by CPI Group (UK) Ltd, Croydon, CR0 4YY

A catalogue record for this title is available from the British Library.

FSC www.fsc.org MIX Paper | Supporting responsible forestry FSC™ C104740

Contents

About the author iv

Getting started v

Action 7

Description 21

The senses 39

Introspection 58

Dialogue 68

Now where? 82

About the author

Chris Youles is an Assistant Head Teacher with 20 years of experience. He has been an English Lead, a writing moderator and a Specialist Leader in Education, working with schools across his county to improve their writing standards. Chris is also an educational author, and he has written three books on writing: *Sentence Models for Creative Writing* (John Catt Educational), *Sentence Models for Non-Fiction Writing* (John Catt Educational) and *Teaching Story Writing in Primary* (Bloomsbury). Chris is an experienced provider of professional development and has delivered workshops to improve English standards across his country. In the past, he has written for Radio 4 and now spends his time starting and never finishing writing the great novel. Chris currently lives and works in Taiwan and divides his time between blogging about writing and failing to go to the gym.

Getting started

How to write a story

Do you want to write a story? Perhaps your teacher has said you have to write one...

What's your first step?

First, you need to decide what the story is about.

- An alien invasion?
- A quest to find a magic sword?
- An epic fight with an ancient, evil creature?
- A heroic journey across a mysterious land?

Stories like these have been told for thousands of years, but that doesn't mean you can't find a fresh way to tell them again.

For example, the story of a battle between a hero and an evil creature is one we've been telling as long as we have been telling stories. This ancient tradition is as old as stories like *Beowulf*, an epic poem written in Old English between the 8th and 10th centuries AD, which tells of him fighting monsters and dragons, or the *Epic of Gilgamesh*, a story over three thousand years old, that has two boss fights! And it continues today – just check the cinema listings to see the same stories being told about heroes going on quests to defeat a villain!

Once you have your story idea, what do you need next?

- A character (or characters).
- A main setting (or world).

All stories need a main character and a cast of interesting people they meet along the way.

You will also need to decide on where your story takes place. Is it in a big city? A faraway magical land? Or on another planet? Wherever you choose, it's important to fill that land with lots of details to make your reader not just **see** the words on the page but **experience** being there.

Once you have your character and a setting, you need to think about what the characters are going to do in your story. To do this, you will need:

- A goal for your character (what your character wants, e.g. to defeat the aliens, to collect the sword, to defeat the ancient monster, to reach the destination).
- Lots of obstacles (things that get in the way of your main character).

Once you have these ideas all fleshed out and ready to go, there is one final thing you need:

- Words.

Or, more, specifically, sentences made up of words – lots and lots of them.

(Unfortunately, just chucking random words on the page won't work.

Fish, aluminium, sausage.

Not a very exciting story, is it?)

Let's use an average book length of 80,000 words and an average sentence length of 15 words.

- Number of sentences = Total words ÷ words per sentence.
- Number of sentences = 80,000 words ÷ 15 words per sentence.
- Number of sentences = approximately 5333 sentences.

Therefore, the average novel-length book likely contains somewhere in the range of 4000 to 7000 sentences.

Now, luckily for you, in school, you are not being asked to write a whole novel (unless your teacher's a tyrant). Most of the time, you will be asked to write a few pages. If you fill up three pages of an A4 exercise book with a story, you would have approximately 50 sentences.

Just 50 sentences. That doesn't sound so bad now, does it?

But what sentences? As a teacher, I have often seen my students eagerly develop plans for their stories only to get stuck when it comes to turning their ideas into sentences and their sentences into paragraphs.

Here's where this book will serve as your guide to writing amazing stories. Using this book means that the next time you need to start describing your setting or a character, you can turn to the relevant section in the book and instantly generate great ideas for your sentences.

So, how does it work?

How to use this book

Let's say you've got your story all planned out.

- **Story idea:** An alien invasion of Earth.
- **Setting:** The local park where an alien capsule has crash-landed.
- **Character:** Jack (aged 9).
- **Character goal:** Jack wants to investigate the crashed ship.

Now you want to write the scene where Jack approaches the alien capsule, but you aren't sure how to do it.

Writers only have four choices for each sentence or paragraph:

- **Action**: things happen.
- **Description**: settings, characters, objects and senses.
- **Introspection**: thoughts and feelings.
- **Dialogue**: characters speaking out loud.

This book is split into these four sections.

When choosing a sentence pattern, you can turn to the section of the book that you want to get a sentence idea from.

In this case, I want to start with an action so I can turn to the action section on page 7.

Looking at the action section, I can choose to use any of the sentence patterns in this section.

For my alien invasion story, I will use a **2 actions** sentence (page 9).

In this book, the sentence pattern example is:

Daniel ran into the woods and scrambled into the undergrowth.

I need to think carefully about my own story to ensure I use the sentence structure effectively. My character, Jack, will be nervous as he approaches a crashed alien ship, so I will try to show that through his actions and my verb choices. He will move quietly, slowly and also perhaps hide, to observe the crash site.

I will change the sentence content like this:

Jack crept silently towards the crash site and hid behind an old oak tree.

I can now use my own ideas or continue looking for sentence patterns.

Another idea is to plan out a variety of sentence types before writing the paragraph. For example, I could choose to use sentences in this order:

1. Action
2. Description
3. Dialogue
4. Introspection

Each of those has lots of great sentence patterns to build on in this book.

When I have finished, then I will hopefully have an effective opening scene such as this:

> *Jack crept silently towards the crash site and hid behind an old oak tree. The air was thick with a metallic scent and scorched grass, and a strange silver dome shimmered in the centre of the park. 'This is way cooler than going to school,' he whispered to himself, his heart thumping. He knew he'd be grounded for a month, but his curiosity about the strange object was overwhelming.*

You can see how these sentences match the order of lenses I chose.

- **Action**: *Jack crept silently towards the crash site and hid behind an old oak tree.*
- **Description**: *The air was thick with a metallic scent and scorched grass, and a strange silver dome shimmered in the centre of the park.*
- **Dialogue**: *"This is way cooler than going to school," he whispered to himself, his heart thumping.*
- **Introspection**: *He knew he'd be grounded for a month, but his curiosity about the strange object was overwhelming.*

What is a sentence?

Before we get stuck into the story writing part, it's important to revise what a sentence is.

A **sentence** is a complete thought or action that has a **subject** and a **predicate**.

The **subject** is who or what the sentence is about.

The **subject** tells us who or what is the person, place, or thing that is doing an action or being described.

- *The **dog** ran.*
  The dog is the subject – it's doing the action.
- *My **teacher** smiled.*
  The teacher is the subject – she's doing the smiling.
- ***London** is a big city.*
  London is the subject – it's what we're talking about.

The subject can be a single word or a group of words, but it's always the **who** or **what** of the sentence.

The **predicate** is what happened in the sentence.

The **predicate** tells us what the subject is doing or being. It's the action part or the descriptive part of the sentence – all the information in the sentence that isn't the subject.

- *The dog **ran all the way to the park**.*
  This part tells us what the dog did.
- *My teacher **smiled at the class**.*
  This tells us what the teacher did.
- *London **is a big city**.*
  This tells us what London is.

The predicate always includes a verb (an action word) and everything that comes after it.

Putting it all together

To make a complete sentence, you need to put a subject and a predicate together.

Subject: *My friend*

Predicate: *built a cool Lego spaceship.*

Complete sentence: *My friend built a cool Lego spaceship.*

You can't have one without the other to make a complete thought. The subject tells us who, and the predicate tells us everything else.

How to use the sentence visual models

Some words in the model can be replaced: for example, in this one 'and' could be changed to 'then'.

WHAT? + WHAT? + and + WHAT?

The girl laughed, picked up her hat and left the room.

_____, _____ and _____.

The blank space is for the word or words you are going to use in your sentence.

Pay attention to the punctuation you need to use. Here you need a comma.

Action

What is the purpose of action in story writing?

Imagine your main character is jumping from a bridge to land on the top of a passing train, or maybe they are swimming away from a bloodthirsty shark.

Action is a term used to describe all the exciting things that are happening in your story.

The purpose of an action sentence is to make your writing dynamic and show what's happening in your story. It drives the story forward and helps the reader picture the events.

Without action, your story would end up as endless description.

Using action to drive your character towards what they want (their goal) and then stuff getting in the way (obstacles) will make your story more exciting to read.

No one wants to read only about how the hero and villain hate each other. Your reader wants to read about them battling it out. This is called **conflict**, and is essential for great storytelling.

Action, 1, 2, 3!

One-action sentences

Daniel ran into the woods.

In our stories, we want our characters to be doing stuff. Action sentences can make your story burst into life and give your reader a really clear picture of what's going on.

We can describe what's happening in a simple action sentence.

Being a writer is like being a film director, but instead of telling your actors to run, you use the words on the page to show what your characters are doing.

A simple action sentence is like a single instruction: *The boy ran.*

Sentence structure

WHO? + WHAT?

Daniel ran into the woods.

____________ + ____________.

Examples

The girl froze.
Mirembe slapped the tentacle away from her face.
Jessica threw her cup of tea at the wall.

Top tip

If you want a short, impactful sentence, you can just write 'Daniel ran.'

Two-action sentences

Daniel ran into the woods and scrambled through the undergrowth.

A more exciting way to write is to link two actions together. Just like a film director asking the actors to do two things, as a writer you can put two actions together. It helps the reader see exactly what happens, step by step. It can give the reader a clearer picture of what is happening and add drama.

Here's an example:

Simple action: *The superhero jumped.*

Linked actions: *The superhero jumped into the air and slammed into the villain.*

Linking the actions *jumped into the air* and *slammed into the villain* makes the scene clearer and more exciting. It tells the reader exactly how the superhero moved.

Sentence structure

WHO? + WHAT? + and WHAT?

Daniel ran into the woods and scrambled through the undergrowth.

______________ and ______________.

Examples

The boy ran into the woods and hid behind an old oak tree.

The guard slammed the door shut and locked it.

Three-action sentences

Daniel ran into the woods, scrambled through the undergrowth and hid behind a tree.

A three-action sentence is a sentence that links three distinct actions together. This provides an even clearer and more detailed picture for the reader.

Here's an example:

The superhero jumped into the air, slammed into the villain and knocked him off his feet.

This sentence has three actions: *jumped*, *slammed* and *knocked*.

Linking three actions together is great because it adds more detail and drama. The reader knows exactly what happened first, second and third.

Also, more actions in a short space can make the scene feel fast-paced and exciting, drawing the reader right into the moment. It gives a more precise and detailed account of the event, making the scene more vivid.

Sentence structure

WHO? + WHAT? + WHAT? + and WHAT?

Daniel ran into the woods, scrambled through the undergrowth and hid behind a tree.

______________, ___________ and ___________.

Examples

The boy ran into the woods, darted through the shadows and hid behind an old oak tree.

The guard pushed her into the cell, slammed the door shut and locked it.

Lots and lots and lots of action

Arina stumbled through the desert, vultures circled overhead, her feet sank into the deep sand and the sun burnt down on her back, until at last she reached a sand dune so high, so wide that she slumped to the ground, resigned to her fate.

Sometimes, you can write a long sentence that links a whole list of events together. This is a brilliant way to create a scene that feels like it's unfolding all at once, giving the reader a vivid and detailed picture. It's like describing everything you can see and hear in a single moment.

This long sequence of actions also helps the reader understand the timeline of events. They know exactly what happened, and in what order.

Let's look at this example, which shows lots of things happening at the same time:

Arina stumbled through the desert, vultures circled overhead, her feet sank into the deep sand and the sun burnt down on her back, until at last she reached a sand dune so high, so wide that she slumped to the ground, resigned to her fate.

In this one sentence, there are seven actions and events that occur:

1. *Arina stumbled through the desert.*
2. *Vultures circled overhead.*
3. *Her feet sank into the deep sand.*
4. *The sun burned down on her back.*
5. *She reached a sand dune.*
6. *She slumped to the ground.*
7. *She was resigned to her fate.*

Linking these actions together creates a sense of urgency and excitement. Just be careful to use commas and words like *and* correctly, so your sentence doesn't become a confusing jumble.

Sentence structure

WHO? + WHAT? + WHERE? (repeated and mixed up)

Himaja leapt over the fence, her hands and legs scraping on the metal, the flames touching at her back behind, the stench of black smoke filling her lungs and the deafening sound of the explosion ringing in her ears.

__________, __________, __________ and __________, __________, __________, __________.

Example

Jax slid down the steep factory vent, razor wire tearing his jacket, the security alarms screaming in his ears and the smell of burning filling his lungs, until he finally dropped onto the cold concrete floor, freezing, defeated and surrounded by blinding spotlights.

Three short actions

Collapsing, crying, crumbling, Robyn fell to the floor in despair.

Why waste time with lots of description or overly complicated sentences? Just pick the three actions you want your character to do and stick them in a sentence. This creates instantaneous, exciting action that will get your reader's heart thumping.

Sentence structure

WHAT? + WHAT? + WHAT? + WHO?

Darting, twisting, pushing, the boy ran through busy streets.

__________, __________, __________, ______________________.

Examples

Crashing, burning, tumbling, the castle tower fell to the ground.

Roaring, screaming, laughing, Year Five ran onto the playground.

Reading, writing, thinking: -ing sentences

Scrambling up the rope, Suneil flung himself over the wall.

The -ing form of a verb is a great tool for adding extra detail to your sentences and linking actions together.

Imagine you're trying to tell a full story in just one sentence. Words that end in -ing can give you more information about what's happening.

However, a sentence that starts with an -ing word can sometimes sound a bit odd, like it's not finished.

Think about a story that begins this way:

Running into the school hall, *Dante.*

It sounds like a fragment or incomplete thought, doesn't it? It feels like the sentence is missing the main point. It leaves you wondering what Dante did. Throw himself into a vat of custard? Do a roly-poly across the stage? What did Dante do? Tell me!

That's because a sentence always needs a main action word – a verb – that shows us what someone is doing. To fix the sentence, you just need to add a main verb that completes the thought.

Running into the school hall, *Dante* ***did*** *a roly-poly across the stage and* ***landed*** *in a giant vat of custard.*

Phew! Now we know what Dante did. The -ing word *running* is a great way to start the sentence, but the main actions, *did* and *landed*, are what make the sentence complete.

Sentence structure

-ING FORM + WHO? + WHAT?

Landing in a heap, the boy collapsed on the ground.

________________, ____________________.

Examples

Falling into the icy water, Jennie began to hyperventilate.

Crashing into the wall, the helicopter burst into a ball of flames.

Top tip

You can play around with the sentence order and put the **-ing verb** *in different positions.*

WHO? + WHAT? + -ING FORM?

The boy collapsed on the ground, landing in a heap.

-ING FORM? + -ING FORM? + WHO? + WHAT?

Laughing and crying, Gill sat down on her bed with a bump.

Short and sweet

The girl reached the edge of the clearing. Run. Run, she thought.

Writing sentences using just one or two words can be really powerful. It makes your reader stop in their tracks and really pay attention to the words you have picked.

Imagine you're reading a story, and everything is moving fast. The hero is in a big fight.

Suddenly you reach a one word sentence...

Disaster.

That single word makes you freeze and pay attention.

Short sentences make the action feel more exciting and powerful. They grab your attention and make the important moments stand out.

Sentence structure

ONE-WORD SENTENCE(s) + WHAT?

Clapping. Cheering. Happiness. Laughter bounced off the walls and filled the room with joy.

_____. + _____. + _____. + _______________.

WHAT? + ONE-WORD SENTENCE(s)

Laughter bounced off the walls and filled the room with joy. Clapping. Cheering. Happiness.

_______________. + _____. + _____. + _____.

ONE-WORD SENTENCE(s) + WHAT? + ONE-WORD SENTENCE(s)

Laughter bounced off the walls and filled the room with joy. Clapping. Cheering. Happiness. The actors walked to the front of the stage and bowed to the audience.

_______________. + _____. + _____. + _____. + _______________.

Two things happening at the same time

As the train pulled into the station, the sun came out.

In story writing, using 'as' sentences is a great way to make action more exciting by showing two things happening at the very same time. It's a fantastic tool for creating suspense and making your reader feel as though they're right in the action.

1. Show a cause and effect

You can use 'as' to show that one action causes another to happen instantly. This builds tension and shows a direct consequence.

Original: *The hero tripped. The villain grabbed him.*

'As' sentence: *As the hero tripped, the villain grabbed him.*

This connects the two actions, making it feel faster and more dramatic.

2. Describe two simultaneous actions

This is where 'as' really shines. It allows you to describe what a character is doing while something else is happening, which adds layers to your scene.

Original (two separate ideas): *The dragon roared. The knight swung his sword.*

'As' sentence: *The knight swung his sword as the dragon roared.*

This makes the scene more vivid. You can picture the brave knight acting despite the terrifying roar.

3. Build tension and foreshadowing

Foreshadowing is the act of giving clues in your story that build suspense and prepare the reader for a dramatic or significant action later in the plot. Using 'as' can also build suspense by hinting at something about to happen.

'As' sentence: *As he reached for the doorknob, a cold draft swept through the hallway.*

This sentence tells us that at the exact moment he touched the door, something spooky happened, making the reader wonder what's behind it.

Think of 'as' as a way to link your sentences together, creating a sense of movement and energy that keeps the reader on the edge of their seat.

Sentence structure

As + 2 × [WHO? + WHAT?]

As he turned to the window, he knew that he was not alone.

As_____________________, ___________________________.

WHO? + WHAT? + as + WHAT?

*He stopped **as** a new wave of pain hit him.*

_________ as ______________________.

More than two things happening at the same time

Think of a movie scene where everything is happening at once. The hero is fighting a bad guy when a storm starts, and an explosion occurs.

Using 'as' **three** times lets a writer do that with words. It's a special trick to cram three different actions into one sentence, making the scene feel fast, chaotic and exciting.

For example, instead of saying:

> *The superhero flew through the air. A storm started. A bomb blew up.*

You can use the three times 'as' trick to make it more powerful:

> **As** *lightning sliced across the sky, as the buildings below her burst into flames,* **as** *she raced through the night sky, she knew that her time might be up.*

See how the action is happening all at once? It creates a vivid picture in your mind and makes the action explode right off the page.

Examples

As the rain lashed down the street, as the rats scurried through the alleyways, as the shadows of the night grew long, the witch arrived at the city gate.

As the wind roared, as the rain fell, as the city grew dark, the creature emerged from its lair.

Where? Where? Where? The power of prepositions

Through the tunnel and over the train tracks, the gang ran desperately towards the exit.

Prepositions are words like 'under', 'on', 'in', 'over' and 'through'.

Using prepositions in your writing is like giving your reader really clear directions. They show your reader exactly what to look at in your story and where it is happening.

See it through the character's eyes

Instead of telling your reader what's happening from above, like a narrator floating in the sky, you can show it and put the reader right inside your character's head. When you describe the scene as the character sees it, it makes the story more exciting and real.

Telling: *A witch was standing in the middle of a street.*

Showing: *The girl's eyes widened as a dark figure stepped out from behind the corner – a witch.*

Using *from behind* lets the reader see the witch just as the girl does – out of nowhere.

Using prepositions ensures that the actions taking place aren't confusing, but instead are precise for your reader.

Think of prepositions as powerful words that guide your reader's eyes and make them feel like they're right there, experiencing the story with your character. They help you build a clear and vivid picture without just telling your reader what they should see.

Sentence structure

WHO? + WHAT? + WHERE?

The girls scrambled up the bank.

__________ WHERE _________.

WHO? + WHAT? + WHERE? + WHERE?

The girls scrambled up the bank through the long grass.

________________ WHERE + WHERE.

WHO? + WHAT? + WHERE? + WHERE? + WHERE?

The girls scrambled up the bank, through the long grass, past a line of trees.

________________ WHERE + WHERE + WHERE.

WHO? + WHAT? + WHERE? + and WHAT? + WHERE?

The girls scrambled up the bank and crawled through the long grass.

______________ WHERE + and + WHERE _____________.

Examples

Indy cut through the undergrowth with his machete and made his way up towards the temple.

The plane streaked across the sky and hurtled towards the sun.

Description

What is the purpose of description in story writing?

Once you have the idea for your story and your main character is running around in the world you've created, it's sometimes important to slow everything down and describe it for your reader.

But be careful not to describe everything in too much detail.

> *The ceiling-mounted smoke detector Model No. SA320WN, requiring two AA-cell batteries for optimal operation, emitted a single, high-frequency chirp at precisely 06:58:34 A.M., signaling its low-power state. Jerry rolled off his memory foam, king-sized mattress and onto the beige cut pile carpet.*

If you describe everything in too much detail, your reader is likely to become bored (unless they're a big fan of smoke alarms).

When choosing what to describe, think carefully about what is important to the story:

- An important setting.
- An important character.
- An important object.

However, what happens if we remove all the description to make it faster and more exciting?

> *The man went to the building. He had a thing with him. He opened the door and walked inside. The room was not big. Something was on the table. The man looked at it. He moved his hand. A sound happened. Then he put the thing down and left.*

If you rush and don't describe anything, your story feels like a fast blur. But if you slow down too much to describe every single tiny thing, your reader might get bored. Get the balance right.

How to write strong settings

What is the setting of a story?

A setting is where your story takes place. This may be on top of a snowy mountain, on an alien planet or in a magical world inhabited by talking plants who are all named Simon.

When thinking about a setting, as a writer, you must decide:

- When is your story set? (the time period, e.g. 1980s.)
- What is the 'big picture' setting? (e.g., New York, USA or Mars.)
- What is the specific place for this scene? (e.g. in the woods, a castle or an abandoned building.)

Top tip

A novel often has many specific settings, but it's much easier to pick one place and explain it well if you are writing a shorter story.

Wherever you decide to set your story, your setting has three main jobs: to orient your reader, to activate the viewpoint and to build atmosphere – positive or negative.

Orienting your reader: Where am I?

> *The man walked into the place. As the man walked around the place, he looked at all the things.*

What's missing? You've probably noticed that there is no description. A lack of description is disorientating and confusing, leaving your reader scrabbling in the dark, trying to comprehend your story.

Your job as a writer is to quickly orient your reader to new settings. It is normally best to do this at the start of your scene. You don't want your reader to be on page five of your story before you tell them, 'Oh yeah by the way, it's set in a hot air balloon.'

Establishing the setting and giving great descriptions of it will help orient the reader and make them feel like they are there.

The man walked into the jungle. The air was hot and humid. Around him the constant drone of insects let him know he was not alone. A green canopy of leaves and gigantic kapok trees blocked the sunlight and bathed the path in an eerie shadow.

Top tip

By using authentic words from a real-world setting (like kapok), you can really bring the scene to life, and the world you are writing seems so much more real.

Activate the viewpoint: How does this setting make the character feel?

A story's point of view can be thought of as asking the question 'Whose story is this?' If you think about J.K. Rowling's *Harry Potter* series, the books are all mainly told from the character Harry's point of view. The reader sees what he is seeing, hears what he hears, feels what he feels and it is his head that we are allowed a peek into to hear his thoughts. Once you, as the writer, decide on the setting, you need to think about how your main character feels when they enter it. Our vocabulary choices, the details we decide to reveal about the setting and the atmosphere we build in our setting are all decided by our character's personality and perspective.

We then write the setting so that it reflects this. Compare the different viewpoints below.

A character who feels at home in the forest

In the heart of the ancient forest, Serena made her way swiftly past trees as old as time, their branches creating a canopy through which shafts of sunlight broke, casting a warm glow on the moss-covered ground below. The air was heavy with the scent of earth and pine, and it wrapped around her like a comforting embrace as she ventured deeper into the woods.

A character who is scared of walking in the forest

Within the heart of the forest, the ancient trees loomed like towering giants, their branches entwined in a sinister dance that cast eerie shadows on the ground. Serena's footsteps echoed like haunting whispers through the paths. Each rustle of a leaf underfoot made her heart beat faster. The air hung heavy with a chilling stillness, and a shiver ran down her spine as she ventured deeper into the woods.

Build an atmosphere

First, decide on the atmosphere you wish to create: horror, foreboding, magical, fantastical, tense, gothic, dystopian, utopian, historical, etc.

Next, choose precise words that enhance your chosen atmosphere. The second example above uses words like 'loomed', 'towering giants', 'haunting', 'chilling' and 'stillness'.

Then, research and add setting details that add to the atmosphere. These could be objects, the weather, or the time period in which the story takes place. Don't forget to slow your pace to add more description, giving yourself time to build the atmosphere.

Add your character's feelings (inside or out), such as 'her heart beat faster' and 'a shiver ran down her spine.' If you want to challenge yourself, you can incorporate symbolism by using an object, character or colour, or create foreshadowing by hinting at events that will occur later in the story through the setting.

Top tip

Inside feelings are when the writer states what the character is feeling, such as 'Jean felt devastated.' Outer feelings are the physical effects of that feeling that a character shows or can't control, such as 'Jean's mouth crumpled and her shoulders sagged.'

Three is the magic number!

Above the fireplace was a large oil painting of a wolf, the room was lined with dusty bookcases and on one shelf sat a large glass display cabinet with a beady-eyed, dead crow in it.

Stop! Look! Listen! See how a pattern of three helps make your writing stand out and grab your reader's attention? This is a great trick to use when writing a setting description. Imagine the setting that you want to describe. Think about the atmosphere you want to create. Now, start by noting down all the things – so, nouns – you can think of that you would find in this place.

You can write them out on a sheet like this. Having an image or video of the setting to work from will really help you here.

Think of the setting and write a thing you might see in each box.

Example: Beach setting

sand	water	seas	horizon	bathers	dolphins	fish
swimmers	boats	waves	surfers	sandcastles	shells	seaweed
crabs	footprints	rocks	sea turtles	sun	seagulls	towels

Now think about where your beach is and what sort of atmosphere you want to create:

- **Where:** Beach in Bali (Indonesia).
- **Atmosphere:** Positive

Expand the nouns into noun phrases

Look at the things you've picked. Now we can add an adjective or adjectives to them to make noun phrases. I want it to be positive and set in Bali (Indonesia), so I may not use seagulls, as that reminds me of an English beach or the time seagulls attacked me for my egg mayonnaise sandwich in a hospital car park in Worthing (true story!).

sparkling, tropical waters	**calm** seas
bobbing boats	**pro**-surfers
golden sands	**endless** horizon

Add some action

Now we can say what some of these things are doing by adding verbs.

sparkling, tropical waters	calm seas
bobbing boats	pro-surfers **navigating the waves**
golden sands	endless horizon

Pick three

Now you can pick three of them and put them together into a pattern of three sentence.

> *There were golden sands, sparkling, tropical waters and pro-surfers navigating the waves.*

Sentence structure

WHAT? + WHAT? + WHAT?

The cave was dank, dirty and thick with the stench of death.

______________, ______________ and __________________.

Examples

The grotto had piles of toys, elves at the workbenches and a sprinkle of magic in the air.

The cave had blood-splattered walls, gnawed animal bones on the floor and the stench of death.

Orient the reader

On the horizon was the elven forest, to the east was the Aatian Sea, and behind him were the rolling mountains he had just left.

When introducing a new setting to the reader, it is useful to create a quick mental image so they understand where the story is set.

Sentence structure

WHERE? + WHAT?

In front of her were tropical palm trees, behind her was the Pacific Ocean and above her was the baking midday sun.

____________, ____________ and _______________.

____________, ____________, ______________ and _______________.

Examples

In front of her was the castle door, to the right was the guard tower and to her left was a collection of ramshackle huts.

Above her was a verdant canopy of leaves, around her were the sounds of tropical birds and in front of her was the seemingly endless rainforest.

Useful vocabulary

- North, East, South, West
- On the horizon
- In the distance
- In front/Behind
- Above/Below
- To the right/left
- In the heart of
- At the edge of
- In the midst of
- Nestled between
- Surrounded by
- Overlooking

Top tip

This is a great way to learn about and use prepositions and prepositional phrases!

Top to bottom and bottom to top

> *Under the midday sun, the stone tower stood on the mountain top and below it ran the valleys and rivers of Riverford.*

Imagine the movie's camera starting at the top of the setting and then panning down. This gives your reader a strong visual image of your setting.

Or, the camera starts at the bottom and pans up to the top.

> *The valleys and rivers ran through Riverford, a stone tower stood on the mountain top above it and the midday sun beat down upon all.*

Sentence structure

WHAT? + WHAT? + WHAT?

__________, __________ **and** ______________.

You can think of it this way:

__________,

____

and ______________.

Examples

The sunlight spilt down from the hills, weaving its way through the trees and fields.

An old shopping trolley sat in the canal, the abandoned factory stood above it and the eerie glow of the moon shone above it all.

Top tip

This could also be used to describe a tall building.

At the top of the palace there was a large red flag fluttering in the wind, the building itself had over a hundred gold-framed windows and a large foreboding moat surrounded it.

....

Zoom in/Zoom out

The man lay on the small wooden raft, floating on the endless seas, under the inky night skies.

Again, imagine you are a movie director and have control of the camera. Start with a wide shot and zoom your camera in towards your main character. Or, you start with a close-up of your main character, and then you pull the camera back to reveal more and more of the setting. In writing, these are called **Zoom ins** and **Zoom outs**. They are a great way of revealing a setting to your reader.

Sentence structure

Zoom in

WHERE? + WHERE? + WHERE + WHO?

In the middle of the empty field, beneath an ancient oak tree, the woman crouched behind the wall.

__________, ______________, ________________, ______________.

Zoom out

WHO? + WHERE? + WHERE? + WHERE?

The woman crouched behind the wall, beneath an ancient oak tree, in the middle of the empty field.

__________, ______________, ________________, ______________.

Examples

The mountains stretched across the skies, a winding path cut through the snowy plains to the peak, the traveller stood at the foot of the path.

The traveller stood at the foot of the winding path that cut through the snowy plains to the mountains that stretched across the skies.

Amplification: Turn it up to 11!

The storm outside was awful: thunder boomed across the sky, lightning slashed through the darkness, heavy sheets of rain pounded the sodden earth.

The purpose of this sentence is to take a single idea, plug it into your guitar amplifier, and blast it out. In the sentence above, we have a simple idea – the storm is awful. Then we take the idea of it being **awful** and provide numerous great descriptions to show why it's so bad. To do this, we make a simple statement, then use a **colon** to start listing everything that makes it **awful** or **magical** or **deadly**...

Sentence structure

WHO? + WHAT? Or WHO? + WHAT? + WHAT?

____________**:** ________________________**.**

Examples

The smell was terrible: toxic fumes filled the air, and a sickening foul odour filled the room.

The room was magical: sparkling, mysterious lights lit up the ceiling, fluttering across it.

Top tip

You can add one more description, two more or as many descriptions as you want.

Change it up! Other types of amplification

Don't forget you can also amplify any other type of description, including the senses.

For example, amplified sounds:

The jungle was full of animal noises: the shrieks of birds and gibbons were howling from the trees above, and the constant scratching of the insects and bugs was all around him.

How to create a character

When your teacher gives you a character sheet (a piece of paper with blanks for name, job, etc.), you might invent a character that sounds super cool.

- **Name:** Tony the amazing ninja hamster.
- **Height:** Three inches high (please don't email me to say your hamster is taller).
- **Job:** Ninja.
- **Personality:** Funny, crazy and shy (all at once!).
- **Looks:** Pink fur with a diamond shaved on his back.

This is a fun start, but when you start writing your story you might get so excited about the action that you completely forget about your own character sheet.

Do you remember the hamster's height (or a close guess at its height)? You say Tony is three inches high, but then you write about him driving a normal car with no hamster car driving adaptations, like three foot-long platform boots (™, I am open to Dragon's Den investors on this one).

The amazing detail you created is totally forgotten and doesn't matter to the story.

Top tip

Instead of just checking things off a list, a great writer asks: 'How does this detail make my character more interesting or help my story?'

If your character is three inches high, then the story should be about the problems or solutions that arise from that. Being three inches high would mean that the character wouldn't be able to drive that car, but they would be able to sneak under locked doors.

What should we describe?

Your teacher might ask you to add more details to your character, like this:

She had brown eyes, long raven-black hair, blue dungarees and a checked shirt.

This is like taking a quick photo for the reader. It helps them build a picture in their head, which is good. But a great description does much more than just list colours and clothes.

The purpose of a character description

The best descriptions give the reader clues about the character's personality, not just state their clothing size.

A standard description tells us what they look like.

A great description tells us what they are like inside and how they act. Or it will hint at a mysterious personality to engage the reader's curiosity. Look at the example below, and see how the man's size may feel intimidating and how his coat and cane add a sinister feeling.

> *Lord Hilton filled the room with his enormous frame; his long, black velvet coat brushed the floor, and in his right hand, he held a long black cane with the head of a wolf.*

Sometimes writers only describe a character with a few details: *The man had a long, curly moustache.*

That's it. Why? Because they want the reader to imagine everything else about the character. You get to fill in the blanks.

On the other hand, some writers tell you everything, down to the exact size of their shoe. That makes the story stop, and it can bore the reader because they want to use their own imagination.

Before you write any description, ask: ***What details about my character actually matter to the story?***

Is their purple hair important because it makes them easy to spot in the snow? Is the scar on their face important because they are hiding from the monster that gave it to them?

If a detail doesn't help the story or show the character's feelings, skip it. Leave a few blank spaces so your reader can use their own imagination. Remember, it's frustrating when a movie character doesn't look like the person you imagined from the book. You want your reader to have fun imagining, too.

Single feature

The black, gloved fist knocked on the door.

Is there a single clothing feature that is part of their character? An item that hints at a character's type? The character with a black, gloved fist knocking on my door sounds a lot scarier than a character wearing a pink tutu and a leopard skin coat. Or is there a single detail of their physical appearance that you could use? A long scar running down their face, or beady eyes?

Sentence structure

WHO? + WHAT?

The man had a narrow, pointy face.

______________ + ________________.

Examples

The old woman had a large, jolly smile on her face.

The new teacher walked into the classroom wearing an oversized pink beret.

The king wore a long purple robe.

Double and triple features

The shopkeeper had warm, grey eyes, long fingernails that she softly clicked on the table in front of her and wore a peacock-blue velvet coat.

Sometimes a single feature isn't enough, and you want to use two or three important details to add that extra depth of description to your character.

Sentence structure

WHO? + WHAT? + WHAT? + WHAT?

His sun-weathered neck, marked by an anchor tattoo, disappeared into the frayed collar of a thick, woollen sweater.

______ + ______ + ______ + ______.

Examples

She wore oversized glasses that magnified her eyes, and her hair was pulled back tightly with a single velvet ribbon.

The young man's shiny black boots clicked loudly on the floor, matching the sharp crease of his ironed trousers and the silver watch chain glinting across his vest.

Let's all do the congeries!

> *His head was covered in a thick layer of fuzzy grey hair, his eyebrows sprang from his eyes like arrows, his ears were overly large and protruded from his head like satellite dishes, his lips were thick and damp, and his eyes were a deep, dark grey like pools of water.*

Sometimes, two or three details will suffice. Sometimes you want your reader to know loads of detail about your main character. To do this, you can pile on detail after detail after detail (in writing, we call this a **congeries**) to create an incredibly rich character description. This time, you can add as many details as you like.

Sentence structure

WHO? + WHAT? + WHAT? + WHAT? + WHAT? + WHAT? + WHAT? + ... etc.

________ + ________ + ________ + ________ + ________

+ ________ + ________ + ________ + ________ **etc.**

Top tip

You can also do this for important settings.

The mysterious shop was a cramped, dusty cavern overflowing with brittle, yellowed maps showing forgotten routes, gleaming brass telescopes aimed, and the faint, lingering smell of old leather and woodsmoke. A single cracked bell above the door failed to ring when you entered, and every shelf sagged under the weight of unlabeled, corked glass bottles, stuffed animals with their dead eyes frozen in fight, and a clock with only a single, backwards-moving hand.

Add some action

Her warm, brown eyes scanned me up and down, making me feel nervous.

The easiest way to make your descriptions powerful is to mix them with action. Don't just stop the story for a long list of facts. Remember, adding description will slow down the story. Building the action in means you get action and description at the same time – two for the price of one! Additionally, the description is now taking an active role in the story, revealing how the character feels or what they are thinking.

Sentence structure

ACTION + DESCRIPTION

DESCRIPTION + ACTION

The detective adjusted her heavy, leather trench coat and sat down at the desk.

____________ + ____________.

Examples

His pale face fell into a pained expression when he saw the broken toy.

The huge man stooped his large frame and climbed into the car.

The renaming friend

Theseus, the hero destined to defeat the Minotaur, entered the labyrinth.

The renaming friend sentence uses a special technique called an **appositive**. An appositive is a word or group of words that sits right next to a noun and gives it a new, extra name or a very specific detail. Think of it as a concise explanation that provides your reader with more information about someone without requiring a new sentence.

How to use the **renaming friend**.

- **Find the noun:** Decide which person, place or thing you want to give a new name to.
  Example: *Theseus.*
- **Add the commas.**
  Example: *Theseus, ____________, entered the labyrinth.*
- **Use the new name:** Put the renaming friend (appositive) right between the commas.
  Example: *Theseus, the hero destined to defeat the Minotaur, entered the labyrinth.*

Notice that if you remove the renaming friend and the commas, the original sentence still makes perfect sense.

Theseus entered the labyrinth.

See? It still works! Ah, friends...

Sentence structure

WHO? + MORE DETAIL + WHAT?

____________, ______________, ____________.

Examples

Sarah, the fastest runner in our school, won the race.

Blake, the school bully, entered the playground with an evil grin on his face.

Top tip

You can use the renaming friend at the end of the sentence, in which case the sentence is punctuated differently.

Theseus entered the labyrinth, determined to face the Minotaur, a ferocious beast with the head of a bull and the body of a man.

We ran past the castle, a cold, dark fortress.

The senses

The senses are a vital part of story writing, and if we can tap into them effectively then it can really add depth to our narrative.

What are the five senses?

- **Sight**: What you see.
- **Sound**: What you hear.
- **Smell**: What you smell.
- **Touch**: What you feel.
- **Taste**: What you taste.

We have all watched a scary movie and felt our heart rate increase or experienced a shiver down our spine (I get the same feeling when I am about to eat the school dinners). Knowing this as a writer means we can use the senses to our advantage by creating a physical reaction in our readers.

Remember that we don't want to rely solely on the sense of sight. Describing the sounds, smells, tastes or touch can be just as powerful.

In every scene, we could focus on a hundred sensory details, but we need to think about the 'why?' and the 'what?'.

Example 1: Too vague

If I write this:

I walked into the bathroom and saw a yucky, gross toilet.

That's boring, right? Words like 'yucky' and 'gross' don't really help your brain paint a picture. They're too vague.

Example 2: Really clear

Now, what if I write this instead? Get ready to feel squeamish and prepare a sick bucket, just in case.

I walked into the bathroom, and the first thing to hit me was the sight of the toilet: full to the brim of a yellow liquid and a thick, brown crust on the seat. Then a pungent, sour smell hit me with such force I could almost feel it trickle down my throat.

Ugh! Did you squirm in your seat? Did you need to use that bucket? That's because I used the senses to manipulate your brain.

- First, I gave you a sight (yellow liquid, brown crust).
- Then, I gave you a powerful smell (pungent, sour).
- Finally, I even hinted at a taste (trickle down your throat).

See? By using strong sensory words, you make the reader feel as though they are right there in the story. That's how great writers bring their worlds to life.

Here is a simple list to think about what your main character might experience through their senses:

- What do they see?
- What do they hear?
- What do they smell?
- What do they touch?
- What do they taste?

Sight

Sight is the most obvious and most used sense, but that doesn't mean we shouldn't use it as writers. By adding what our characters can see around them, we can describe the world they are in, the characters they meet and the objects they use.

When you're describing what your character sees, you have two main tools: **precise nouns** and **adjectives.**

1. The power of a precise noun

Sometimes, one great word is better than using three or four adjectives to describe something.

Instead of writing:

*The **big, brown, scary** dog.*

You can use a precise noun to help the reader see it instantly.

*The **Rottweiler**.*

See how much faster and clearer that is? The word 'Rottweiler' already tells us it's a large, brown and possibly scary (sorry Rottweiler fans...I'm sure they are actually lovely).

2. When to use adjectives

Sometimes, you need to use extra words – adjectives – to describe something. This is especially true if it's something the reader has never seen before or something really important in the story.

Imagine you invent a monster called a 'Gromble'. The reader will have no idea what that looks like if you just write: *The Gromble ran towards me.*

In my writer's head, I know that the Gromble is meant to be terrifying, but my reader might imagine a fluffy, soft creature with big, round eyes.... Ah, lovely, old Gromble. To ensure that I create the desired effect, I need to add more detail. To do this, I need to use **expanded noun phrases** (one or two adjectives next to the nouns) to build a clearer picture.

Feature	What it looks like (adjectives)
head	**dome-shaped** head
skin	**leathery**, **stretched** skin
tentacles	**limb-like** tentacles

Now you can write a really exciting sentence that will give a much clearer image of the Gromble.

The creature climbed out of the pit. Its **dome-shaped head** wobbled, its **leathery skin** was covered in sweat and its **limb-like tentacles** writhed like snakes searching for prey.

Something important in your story

Just as we slow down for important settings or characters to describe them, sometimes we also need to slow down to describe an important object.

Imagine we are about to describe a sword in our story. Is this sword going to be important? If so, we want to slow the pace down and describe it in detail.

> *The sword lay on the beach next to the lake. Its razor-sharp blade was long and curved. The silver handle was engraved with pictures of dragons and mysterious letters from a long-forgotten ancient language.*

This detail informs the reader that the sword holds significance for the story (foreshadowing!).

However, we also have to consider **where** we slow down to describe. If we go into this sort of detail in the middle of an action sequence, then it will ruin the flow.

> *The guard grabbed his sword and swung it at Jak's head. Its razor-sharp blade was long and curved. The silver handle was engraved with pictures of dragons and mysterious letters from a long-forgotten ancient language. Jak ducked.*

In this case, it would be better to leave the description out.

The adjective order rule

When you do decide to use lots of adjectives, English has a rule about the order you must put them in. No one knows why the rule exists, but if you get it wrong, the sentence sounds silly.

Compare these:

- 'The chopping metal ancient large knife.' sounds weird.
- 'The large ancient metal chopping knife.' sounds right.

Here is the secret order you should follow for your adjectives.

1. **Opinion**: useless, amazing, etc.
2. **Size**: e.g., large, tiny, etc.
3. **Age**: e.g., ancient, new, etc.
4. **Shape**: e.g., round, square, etc.
5. **Colour**: e.g., purple, green, etc.
6. **Material**: e.g., metal, leather, etc.
7. **Purpose**: e.g., chopping knife, swimming goggles, etc.

This rule helps you choose the most important details.

Which adjectives should I use?

Does it matter more that the sword is silver (colour) or that it is razor-sharp (opinion)?

To make these decisions, we need to think about our purpose. Let's say it's to describe the English countryside.

The big old brown trees lined the path.

For this sentence, precise nouns would be more effective than a chain of adjectives.

And if you don't know any, then you need to do what all writers do – research!

English oak and common beech trees lined the path.

This second sentence fits the purpose far better than the first.

Don't forget, the last question is whether we need an adjective at all, or if it will slow down the story. Would it be better to just write, *Trees lined the path.*?

Double and triple the sight

The iron-bound chest was covered with dust, locked with a rusty padlock and etched with forgotten symbols.

For this sentence pattern, you need to pick the two or three most important details about the thing that your main character is looking at.

Sentence structure

WHAT? + SIGHT and SIGHT

The bookcase stood against the far wall, dusty and huge.

_______________, _________ and __________.

SIGHT and SIGHT + WHAT?

Dusty and huge, the bookcase stood against the far wall.

_________ and ________, __________________.

WHAT? + SIGHT + SIGHT + SIGHT

The golden key was six inches long, engraved with strange markings and faintly glowing red.

_________________________, _____________ and __________.

Examples

The heavy, velvet curtain was midnight blue and weighted with thick tassels.

A stack of photographs, curled at the edges and bleached by years of sunlight, showed her family in happier times.

A chipped porcelain doll, missing one eye and dressed in a lace gown, sat motionless on the shelf.

Adding action to sights

He took the sword, a long, curved weapon, and put it in his bag.

When you weave descriptive details into a character's action, you are showing the reader the information rather than just telling them. Instead of stopping the narrative to insert a paragraph of description, you move the plot forward while describing the world.

Sentence structure

ACTION + OBJECT DESCRIPTION

Out of his pocket, he produced a long, wooden wand.

ACTION + __________________________.

ACTION + OBJECT + DESCRIPTION

Out of his pocket, he produced a wand, a long, twisted piece of wood that glowed at the end.

ACTION + ______________ + _______________.

Examples

He stomped his heavy, mud-caked boots across the clean carpet.

The captain gripped the worn, splintered wheel tightly, fighting the sudden storm.

The nervous thief pocketed the small, glittering diamond before anyone in the crowd could see.

Show, don't tell

> *A dry scent of linen, the fine grit of gold dust on the floor, and a sarcophagus carved from a single block of basalt – it was the untouched burial chamber.*

You can create an effective 'show, don't tell' description by revealing the senses as **clues**. This helps build tension and suspense in your writing. Your reader will often be ahead of you and excited, as they realise what is about to happen.

Sentence structure

SIGHT 1 + SIGHT 2 + SIGHT 3 + REVEAL

Under the full moon, he saw it standing on the hill: long, black ears, grey matted fur and yellow, pointed teeth – it was a werewolf!

__________ + __________ + __________ + __________.

Examples

The footsteps grew closer, a shadow paused at his bedroom door and the faint sound of muttering crept into the room – the creature was in his house!

Giant footprints covered the ground, bushes and trees had been freshly trampled and the smell of blood and decay hung heavy in the air – it was the T. rex!

Top tip

You can mix this up by using more than one sense.

SOUND + SIGHT + TOUCH + REVEAL

A guttural growl filled the air, a snarling sound crept up on her and its hot breath warmed her neck – it was the wolf!

__________ + __________ + __________ + __________.

....

Repeat after me: Sights

I will find the magic sword. I will unite the kingdom. I will defeat the monster.

Repetition is a brilliant trick that expert writers use to make their writing powerful and memorable. **Anaphora** is the fancy name for this simple writing technique: repeating the exact same word or phrase at the beginning of several sentences or clauses that follow each other. This repetition forces the reader to focus on the repeated phrase and the idea behind it.

Sentence structure

WHAT? + REPETITION + REPETITION + REPETITION

Tito could see: endless blue water, endless blue sky, endless sunshine.

__________ + REPETITION + REPETITION + REPETITION.

REPETITION + REPETITION + REPETITION + WHAT?

Endless blue water, endless blue sky, endless sunshine – Tito was in paradise.

REPETITION + REPETITION + REPETITION + __________.

Examples

The mist climbed over the hill. The mist swallowed the last light of the moon. The mist brought the chill of winter into the room.

They did not run when the earth shook. They did not run when the sirens wailed. They did not run, because they had nowhere left to go.

She understood the journey she had to take. She understood the sacrifices she would have to make. She understood that destiny was calling her name.

Top tip

It's not just sights that you can repeat. It's actually any idea in the sentence: smells, sounds, thoughts, feelings, dialogue, etc.

Sound

It's essential when using description not to rely solely on sights. Sounds – what someone can hear – can also bring a scene to life and add depth to your writing. Using the right sounds to make the reader feel like they are right there in the action.

Imagine you are writing about a giant chasing the hero, and then the giant trips and falls.

> *The giant lost his footing and fell. He landed on the ground, and the whole area shook.*

That tells us what happened, but a giant falling should be loud. The writing feels flat because we can't *hear* the huge impact.

Let's add some sounds.

> *The giant lost his footing and fell. He crashed to the earth with a sound like a hundred trees splintering, followed by an earth-shaking thud that sent an echoing boom across the ground.*

What happened here?

1. 'Crashed' and 'thud' show the extreme volume and force of the impact.
2. 'Splintering' is a descriptive sound **verb**, used to help the reader imagine the force of his body hitting the ground.
3. 'Echoing boom' lets us know just how huge this sound is.

When you read the version with the sounds put in, you don't just see the giant fall. You can hear it as well.

When something important happens, ask yourself:

1. What specific noise does this event make?
2. How can I use sound in this part of my story to bring it to life?

To choose our sounds, we can break them down into simple pairings.

- **loud** or **quiet**
- **audible** or **inaudible**
- **melodic** or **tuneless**
- **soft** or **hard**
- **soothing** or **shrill**
- **still** or **cacophonous**
- **clear** or **muffled**

Crash! Bang! Wallop! Onomatopoeia

The loose floorboard let out a sudden, sharp creak and a faint, muffled thump as the man stepped across the room.

One of the simplest ways to bring a sound into a sentence is through the use of **onomatopoeia**. Onomatopoeia is a fancy word for saying: the word itself sounds like the noise it is describing.

Think of it like this: If you read the word, you can almost hear the noise right in your head.

Sentence structure

ONOMATOPOEIA + ONOMATOPOEIA + ONOMATOPOEIA + ACTION

Crunch, crunch, crunch. The old man walked through the snow towards the mountain.

______________ + ______________ + ______________ + ______________.

Examples

Drip, drip. drip, drip. The sound of the rusty tap leaking filled the house.

Boom! Boom! Boom! The sound of knocking on the door filled the room.

Top tip

Change it up! Use two or three different onomatopoeia sounds to build tension.

Screech! Clank! The car pulled up outside the house.

Clang! Crack! Crash! The sounds of the swords on shields filled the battlefield.

Where's the sound?

A tiny, frightened squeak came from the deep darkness of the tunnel ahead.

Expert writers know that sound doesn't just happen – it **moves**. The way a sound travels tells the reader exactly where the character is, how big the space is and where the danger (or excitement) is coming from. Using sound can help create a mental map for the reader.

Examples

Sound far away

I listen carefully and can hear a distant rumble of thunder.

Sound nearby

An ear-splitting scream exploded right behind me, forcing me to spin around.

Sounds getting further away

The sounds of the horse's hooves disappeared into the distance.

The plane's engine soon became a distant hum as it disappeared into the distance.

Sounds getting closer

The footsteps came closer to his room as the heavy boots thumped down the hallway.

The approaching sirens grew louder and louder.

Sound moves over/around

The sounds of nature rolled over him like a wave.

The sounds of nature flowed around him like a river.

Smell

Did you know that smells are closely connected to your memories? When I smell Lynx Africa (and stale sweat) it transports me instantly back into the memory of my teenage bedroom.

This means that one simple smell can instantly take your character (and your reader) back in time.

Imagine a character walks into a room and smells the damp, cool stone – it might instantly remind them of a spooky holiday cottage they visited years ago.

Don't just write *She smelled something good.*

Be specific. Use precise words to describe exactly what the air smells like.

Scientists have found that we can actually smell about ten different kinds of smells: **fragrant**, **woody/resinous**, **minty/peppermint**, **sweet**, **chemical**, **popcorn**, **lemon**, **fruity (non-citrus)**, **pungent** and **decayed**.

As a writer, you can use these categories to give your reader a powerful sensory clue.

Think about the mood of your scene. If it's a happy scene, use a fragrant smell. If it's a scary scene, use a chemical or decayed smell to make the reader feel worried.

Smell type	Example	What feeling does it give?
Fragrant	Fresh-baked cookies, a new flower	Comfort, happiness
Pungent	Musty air, stagnant water	Danger, disgust, suspense

Top tip

If you can't think of a smell to use, then don't force it – you don't want to have clunky sentences like 'The house smelled like a house.'

Smells you remember

The witches' cottage smelled of gingerbread, warm cinnamon, and a sugar so intensely sweet it prickled the back of their throats.

Think about when you walk into a kitchen or hike through a forest. Before you see anything, your nose tells you exactly where you are. Smells don't just describe a place, they tell your reader how to feel about that place.

Write down your setting (e.g. forest) and then write down three smells it makes you think of: for example, pine trees, dank earth or the smell of autumn.

Sentence structure

SMELL? + WHAT?

________________ + ____________________.

Examples

The wet moss, dank earth and fresh pine smell filled his nostrils.

The fresh sea air tickled her nose with its salty fingers.

Top tip

You can use the idea of the air or a breeze carrying the smell to your character.

AIR + SMELL?

The soft breeze carried with it the fresh smell of spring.

In the air, the sweet smell of freshly baked bread drifted into the room.

....

Touch

Sometimes when we write, we forget about the sense of touch, but don't get touchy about it (sorry...this is the worst joke yet).

Touch is one of the most important senses. When your character touches something, you can make your reader feel it too.

When we use the sense of touch, it isn't just about saying something is soft or rough. Using touch is also about how things feel to your character.

Texture

The easiest thing to describe is the texture of an object. This is what it feels like right on your skin.

Instead of writing *The wall was hard.* write:

> *He ran his hand over the stones – they were slick with cold rainwater and covered in fuzzy moss.*

Texture	Examples
Rough/coarse	Sandpaper, tree bark, stone
Bumpy/ridged	Cobbled street, dragon scales, scarring
Smooth/fine	Glass, polished wood, metal
Slippery	Oil, ice, water

Temperature and power

Touch isn't just about texture, it's also about physical feelings.

Use these to show your character's situation:

- Temperature.
- Weight.
- Pain or pressure.

Touch	Example
Temperature	The cold wind whipped at his skin.
Weight	He managed to pick up the shield, but its enormous weight immediately buckled his knees.
Pain or pressure	The rope cut into his wrists and stopped the flow of blood to his fingers.

Terrific textures

The crystal ball felt smooth in his hands.

When your character touches something, it should **change** how they feel. Use touch to evoke emotions in your reader, from shivering to relaxation to wincing. To do this, use the texture of the object.

Sentence structure

WHO? + WHAT? + TEXTURE

Her grandmother's blanket felt rough in her hands.

_______ ___+ __________ + __________.

Examples

He pulled his hand back from the crate's splintered edge.

The worn leather chair felt soft and comfortable against his back.

Touch: How does it make you feel?

Jemima picked up the sword and felt its incredible weight.

When we think about the object our character is interacting with, we should also think about the physical effect it might have on the character. If we don't use touch in our writing it may not make sense. For example, if a young boy picks up a heavy table and we don't describe its weight, then that may feel weird for our reader.

Sentence structure

WHO? + WHAT? + PHYSICAL EFFECT

Joe held the wand, and an exciting tingling sensation filled his hands.

________ + _________ + ___________.

Examples

The glass sliced across her hand, sending a slashing pain rushing through her.

The pendant glowed a deep red, and she could feel it burning her skin.

Taste

Taste is a tricky sense to use, and you don't want to describe your character licking trees and telling the reader, 'Junjie licked the tree, and it tasted like wood.'

Instead, the best way to use taste is when your character is:

- Eating or drinking something.
- Interacting with something in the air.

When you write about taste, you are telling the reader what the character has in their mouth. But it's more than that – you are telling the reader how the food makes the character **feel**.

The power of positive or negative

In your story, you can use taste to evoke a strong emotional response in the reader, either making them feel **really happy** or **grossed out**.

Feeling	Goal	Example
Positive taste	Make your reader feel comfort, warmth or excitement.	The warm stew filled his stomach.
Negative taste	Make the reader feel disgust, danger or pain.	The old meat was so rancid it made her gag.

A quick tip on tastes

There are four main types of taste.

Taste category	What it means	Examples
Sweet	Sugary, delicious, dessert-like.	Syrupy, candied, saccharine
Salty	Like the sea, or crisps.	Briny, savoury
Sour	Acidic, like lemons or vinegar	Tart, vinegary, citrusy, sharp
Spicy	Hot, causing a burning sensation	Fiery, scorching, blistering, volcanic

Never just tell the reader **what** the food is. Instead, tell them **what it feels like** to eat it.

Mix the senses up

The cold, gritty saltiness of the wind whipped her cheeks raw as she watched the grey ocean churn.

(Touch, Taste, Touch, Sight)

The sentence above has touch (*cold, gritty*), taste (*saltiness*), touch again (*whipped her cheeks raw*) and sight (*grey ocean churn*).

We can focus on more than one sense in a sentence, and mixing them up is a good way of revealing more sensory details in one go.

Sentence structure

LOOKS? + SOUNDS? + SMELLS?

It looked revolting. It sounded like a slobbering dog. It smelt like rotten eggs.

________ + ________ + ________.

SIGHT? + SOUND? + SMELL?

Ahead of me, the sands roll out in an endless carpet, the distant sounds of the cries of vultures ring out and the smell of sour sweat from my clothes reminds me of how long I've been in this desert.

________ + ________ + ________.

Top tip

You can mix up as many of the senses as you want in your sentence, but remember that they should be used to create a positive or negative effect and let the reader know how it feels to your character.

Introspection

What is the purpose of introspection in story writing?

OK, you've got your character running around in the world that you've created. As a writer, we now need to show what our character is **thinking** and **feeling**.

Imagine you're out on the school playground, but instead of just watching everyone run around, you could push a pause button and look right inside their heads to see what they're thinking, and into their hearts to find out what they're feeling.

Introspection refers to the moments when a character looks inward, reflecting on their own thoughts, feelings, motivations and internal struggles. It's about revealing the character's inner world to the reader, rather than just their actions or dialogue.

Top tip

One thing to remember is that too much introspection can slow the story down and bore the reader. Being in the character's head the whole time can start to feel like that time you stole your sister's/brother's (delete as appropriate) diary and read it. This is a common writing error when writing in the first person!

Introspection needs to be balanced with external action and dialogue. Every moment of introspection should serve a purpose – to reveal character or advance the plot.

Imagine, instead of just saying that a knight fought a dragon, the story shows the knight thinking, *My knees are shaking, but I have to protect the village!* You learn they're brave even when they're scared.

You see their struggles: characters often have internal conflicts, such as trying to decide what's right or wrong, or fighting off a bad feeling. Introspection shows you these inner battles.

Imagine a character finds a lost wallet, and the story tells us if they keep it or return it.

Introspection would reveal that they were thinking about how much they needed the money versus how bad they'd feel if they didn't return it. Sometimes, the most important things that happen in a story are the big changes inside a character's mind rather than the actual events.

Just remember, a good writer knows when to show you a character's thoughts and when to let the action speak for itself. It's all about making the story exciting and richer, and the characters feel real.

Inside: Feelings

Let's have a good look at what is going on inside our character! What are they feeling?

In these sentences, we can just tell our reader how they are feeling. It's simple, quick and and an easy way of showing their feelings. We can use one feeling or double it with two feelings at the start. Additionally, we can describe what's happening first and then express the feeling.

Sentence structure

FEELING? + ACTION?

Terrified, Jobe entered the dimly lit cave.

FEELING, ______________________.

FEELING? + FEELING? + ACTION?

Terrified and confused, Jobe entered the dimly lit cave.

FEELING + FEELING, ______________________.

WHAT? + FEELING?

Jobe looked around at the shadowy walls of the cave, terrified.

____, FEELING.

WHAT? + FEELING?

Jobe looked around at the shadowy walls of the cave, terrified and confused.

____, FEELING + FEELING.

Top tip

Try to use two unique feelings rather than synonyms for the same feeling.

Terrified and sacred, Jobe entered the dimly lit cave.

'Terrified' and 'scared' are pretty much the same – just that one is a stronger feeling than the other!

Opposing feelings

Determined, but terrified on the inside, Chetana picked up the sword.

Have you ever been on a scary ride? Remember that moment when you are climbing up the steepest part of the rollercoaster and are just about to be launched down at 100 mph? At that moment, we can feel contradictory or opposing feelings – scared **and** excited. Often, our characters will have more than one feeling at the same time. This is a great way of showing our readers the conflict our character may be feeling.

Sentence structure

FEELING + but + OPPOSITE FEELING

FEELING, but FEELING, ________________________.

Examples

Terrified, but excited, Jobe entered the dimly lit cave.

Excited, but nervous, Sam picked up the baseball bat and walked to the pitch.

Inside: Thoughts

'Does he think I'm crazy?' Amy wondered, as she sat down at the table.

The easiest way to write about what your character is thinking is to use a rhetorical question. This is a question that you don't answer. In fact, it's a little bit like a statement in disguise. Look at the sentence above. *Does he think I'm crazy?* is more like a statement of what Amy thinks.

You can use one question, two questions or three questions, and you can play around with the order of your sentence.

Sentence structure

WHO? + WHAT? + 2 × RHETORICAL QUESTIONS

Mira looked him up and down. Why should I trust you? Why should I care what you think?

____________ + __________ + × 2 RHETORICAL QUESTIONS

WHO? + WHAT? + 3 × RHETORICAL QUESTIONS

Mira looked him up and down. Why should I trust you? Why should I care what you think? Who do you think you are?

____________ + __________ + × 3 RHETORICAL QUESTIONS

Top tip

You can also switch it around and start with the questions.

× RHETORICAL QUESTIONS + WHO? + WHAT?

Vampires? Werewolves? Jacek's eyes widened in terror.

× 2 RHETORICAL QUESTIONS + ____________ + __________ .

....

Thoughts: Mixing up the sentence types

This was going to be the fight of his life. Could he really win? What if he lost? 'I must succeed!' he thought.

The four main sentence types are a great way of capturing your character's thoughts.

- Question
- Statement
- Command
- Exclamation

Look at the sentence above again.

This was going to be the fight of his life. Could he really win? What if he lost? 'I must succeed!' he thought.

We have: Statement, Question, Question, Exclamation.

By doing this, we can capture what it's like to be inside our character's mind with all the different thoughts they are having.

In writing, we call this **internal conflict**.

It's like your mind arguing with itself.

You can mix the sentence types to show all sorts of internal conflicts in a character's mind.

Sentence structure

STATEMENT + QUESTION

The last place the wolf had been seen was in the woods. Could he go in knowing this?

______________________ . + ____________________ ?

STATEMENT + QUESTION + STATEMENT + QUESTION

The last place the wolf had been seen was in the woods. Could he go in knowing this? It had long, yellow teeth and was known to eat children. Was this such a great idea?

___________ . + _____________ ? + _____________ . + ______________ ?

QUESTION + EXCLAMATION + QUESTION + EXCLAMATION + QUESTION + STATEMENT

A wolf? How bizarre! Out in the woods? Impossible! Could he go in? He simply must.

__________ ? + _____________ ! + _____________ ? + _____________ ! + __________ ? + _____________ .

Outside: Physical effects

Imagine you are walking alone through a dark forest. It's midnight, and you suddenly hear a strange noise from the darkness around you.

What physical effects might happen to your body?

- Your hand covers your mouth.
- Your heart beats faster.
- Your breathing becomes shallow.

Voluntary versus involuntary effects

The difference between voluntary and involuntary effects of feeling is simple: it's about what you **choose** to do versus what your body does automatically without you telling it to.

- Your hand covers your mouth: voluntary.
- Your heart beats faster: involuntary.
- Your breathing becomes shallow: involuntary.

Voluntary effects are actions your character consciously chooses to perform. They decide to do it to show their feelings, or to hide them. Examples could include:

- **Anger**: Slamming a fist on the table, stomping a foot, crossing arms.
- **Sadness**: Covering your face with your hands, hunching your shoulders, forcing a smile to pretend you're okay.
- **Fear**: Taking a step back, hiding your eyes, whispering.

Involuntary effects are actions your body performs automatically because of a feeling, like reflexes. You can't stop these easily, even if you try. Examples could include:

- **Anger**: Your face turning bright red, your jaw clenching tight, your breathing speeding up.
- **Fear**: Sweating palms, racing heart, eyes widening, trembling.
- **Excitement**: Butterflies in your stomach, fast, shallow breaths, spontaneous laughter.

When you write, use both. The voluntary actions show what the character wants others to see, but the involuntary feelings (like a pounding heart) are the secret signs of the emotion bubbling underneath.

Feeling: Short physical effect

She looked surprised.

Sometimes, in writing, we can tell the reader directly how the character feels. If we do this, then it is best to keep your sentence short and sweet.

Sentence structure

WHO? + WHAT?

He looked relieved.

________ + __________.

Examples

She hesitated.
She took a deep breath.
Ali frowned.
Olivia breathed in sharply.
Greta felt her shoulders tense.
She gasped out loud.
He grinned.

Use your body: Feelings

He threw his hands up in the air in frustration.

Remember those physical effects?

Well, we can use them in our writing to show our characters' feelings.

Take the physical effect and put it into a sentence.

Sentence structure

WHO? + SHORT PHYSICAL EFFECT + WHAT?

Her eyes opened wide in shock.

__________ + __________ + __________.

Examples

His mouth made an 'O' in amazement.

She gasped and curled up into a ball.

His face went purple, and he threw his phone across the room.

Dialogue

What is the purpose of dialogue in story writing?

OK, you've got your setting, and you've got your characters running around in it. Now you need to think about what the characters might say to each other.

This is called **dialogue**.

Great dialogue plays a crucial role in the story. The best writers use dialogue to do more than just let characters talk.

Dialogue has five main jobs in your story.

- **Show character goals**: What does your character want?
- **Reveal conflict**: Make characters argue or disagree (arguments where the characters are fighting about their goals are even more powerful).
- **Advance the action**: Move the plot forward.
- **Show character**: Show the reader what a character is like.
- **Reveal exposition (backstory)**: Drop hints about the past or the world the characters are living in.

Top tips

- ***Find the purpose:*** *Before you write a piece of dialogue, decide which of the five jobs (conflict, action, character, etc.) it needs to do. If it doesn't do a job, delete it.*
- ***Pick apart existing dialogue:*** *When you're reading a book, pick a scene and ask yourself what this character is trying to achieve with this one line?*
- ***Lose the greetings:*** *In real life, we say 'Hello,' but in stories, characters usually get straight to the point to save time.*
- ***Opposing goals:*** *When you write a dialogue scene, give each character something different they want. Their words will clash naturally.*

- ***Use personality:*** *Make your shy character talk quietly, and your loud character use big, dramatic words. You should be able to guess who is talking even without the dialogue tag.*

Show character goals

The simplest way for dialogue to show a goal is when the character just says it. This is usually done to kick off the next part of the plot.

Character's goal examples	Dialogue that reveals the goal
To get inside a specific building.	*'I need to go into that house,' said Sachin. 'I've lost my dog and I think I saw it run in there.'*
To get the other person to hurry up.	*'We need to be on the bus now,' snapped Maya. 'If we miss this one, the whole plan is ruined.'*
To force someone to tell the truth.	*'Don't lie to me, Jasper! Where did you hide the key?'*

Reveal conflict

Dialogue is amazing for showing conflict. This doesn't have to mean a shouting match or an actual punch-up. It means two characters have opposing goals (they want different things).

The Scene: Mirembe wants her father to let her explore the forest with the older children in the village.

Direct conflict (they openly disagree)

'Why can't I explore the forest?' Mirembe asked, her eyes wide with anger.

'The answer is no, now go to your room,' her father replied, his face flushed with frustration.

Hidden conflict (one character is hiding something)

'Why can't I explore the forest?' Mirembe asked, her eyes wide with anger.

'The answer is no,' her father replied.

'Why not?'

'You are too young for the truth,' her father said. For a moment, he looked as if he was going to say something else, but instead slumped into his armchair in silence.

The refusal creates mystery and tension, and the reader wonders what her father is not telling her.

Advance the action

Advancing the action means moving the story on, keeping the plot moving forward. Dialogue should never leave your characters standing around doing nothing. It must lead to a new event.

Dialogue moves the action forward when it:

- **Gives a new goal**:

  'I think we should try and find shelter,' Ruadh said, looking up at the approaching storm.

- **Explains an obstacle**:

  'I can't climb up!' she grunted. 'The walls are too slippery.'

- **Introduces new information**:

  'Don't you know? The whole kingdom has been under a terrible spell since the Ice Queen arrived.'

- **Discusses a solution**:

  'If we work on our own we will never defeat the cyclops, but if we work as a team we may stand a chance.'

Show character

What your character says when things get tricky is a great hint about their personality.

- Does the super-intelligent character become quiet and thoughtful when faced with a problem?
- Does the character with anger issues start screaming, shouting and smashing stuff?
- Does the nervous character talk really fast when they are stressed?

A character's reaction to conflict shows the reader who they are.

Reveal exposition (backstory)

Exposition is just a fancy word for all the background information you need to know, also known as the backstory. What happened before the story started? Has an evil king ruled the land for 10 years? Did your character's dad have a job as an MI5 spy? Did your character have a terrible experience with a snake when they were a child?

Instead of telling the reader everything in one big lump (in writing, this is called an information dump), great writers use dialogue to reveal it in small 'sprinkles' throughout the story.

The easiest trick is to make sure one character knows something the other doesn't. This makes telling the reader about the backstory seem more natural.

Dump (telling)

In this first example, I will dump all the information onto the reader. When you read it, can you see that it feels like the writer is telling you all of this important information?

> *High above the clouds, a young boy named Leo Rocket was busy in his spaceship, the Galaxy Cruiser. Leo had to fly the Cruiser as fast as he could to the green planet called Zorp. He needed to get there quickly because his best friend, his dog Cosmo, had been accidentally teleported to Zorp after leaning on the wrong button at the space station, and Cosmo only had enough oxygen in his space-collar for three more hours, so Leo had to save him fast before the time ran out.*

Dialogue (showing)

In this second example, I will make sure that Leo's goals and obstacles are revealed through dialogue instead. Can you see now how the information feels more natural and comes from our character, Leo, rather than the writer?

> *Leo Rocket gripped the steering wheel of the Galaxy Cruiser so hard his knuckles turned white. In the distance, he could see the green planet Zorp, hanging in the infinite blackness of space.*
>
> *'GALAXY, status check. How far to Zorp?' Leo snapped, his voice tight.*
>
> *A metallic voice replied, 'Distance to Planet Zorp: One hundred thousand parsecs. Estimated time of arrival at current speed: two hours, forty-five minutes.'*
>
> *'That's too slow! Cosmo only has three hours on that collar!' Leo slammed his hand on the throttle.*

Top tip

If a line of dialogue doesn't have a job, you should cut it out. Let's look at an example.

'Hello,' said Sarah.

'Hi,' said Tara.

'What did you have for breakfast?' said Sarah.

'I had cornflakes. What did you have?' said Tara.

This dialogue doesn't reveal anything about our characters (except for the fact that Tara likes cornflakes, but really, who cares) or advance the action, so we don't need it. In fact, in most stories, the author will eliminate the unnecessary greetings and get straight to the point.

Who said what? Simple dialogue

Gerald looked at Arthur and said, 'You must be absolutely barking mad.'

Most of the time, you want to keep your dialogue nice and simple.

1. Who is speaking?
2. What do they say?

Using 'said' is also absolutely fine. Your character doesn't always have to be 'exclaiming', 'growling' and 'grunting'. In fact, 'said' is pretty much invisible to a reader and doesn't get in the way of your excellent dialogue.

You can also switch this around.

1. What do they say?
2. Who is speaking?

'You must be absolutely barking mad,' Gerald said, looking at Arthur.

Sentence structure

WHO? + VERB + DIALOGUE

__________ + __________ + , '__________.'

DIALOGUE + WHO? + VERB

'__________,' + __________ + __________.

Examples

'We have to leave now before the ice breaks,' Amy said.

Amy said, 'We have to leave now before the ice breaks.'

It's not what you say, but how you say it

'That's a terrible idea,' Panchali said angrily.

If you want to reveal how your character feels, then an easy and efficient way is to add an adverb that states how they are feeling.

Sentence structure

DIALOGUE + WHO + VERB + ADVERB

'__________,' + __________ + __________ + __________.

Examples

'That must be the way out,' said Greta excitedly.

'I don't think you want to do that,' said Jacek threateningly.

Adding some action: Dialogue

> *'Look, that must be the Emerald Forest,' said Gina, jumping up and down in excitement.*

Think how bizarre it would be if you were talking with someone and you were both standing completely still.

One way to bring your scenes to life is by adding actions to dialogue, describing what a character is doing while they speak.

When choosing what a character is doing (the action), consider how they are feeling and think of an action or actions that match that feeling – for example, my character is excited, so I will have them jumping up and down). Make sure the feeling matches or it may sound weird: *"I'm so sad," Tina said dancing excitedly around the living room.*

You can also add action to bring the dialogue to life by having your character do something while they are talking.

Sentence structure

DIALOGUE + VERB + WHO? + WHAT?

'__________,' + _________ + _________ + __________.

Examples

'I just give up,' Grace said, collapsing to the floor in a heap.

'There's nothing for you to see here,' Tara said, quickly shoving the map into her backpack.

Top tip

Instead of an action, you can add a physical effect to show how the character is feeling.

DIALOGUE + PHYSICAL EFFECTS?

'How dare you,' he said, his lips pursed.

'You'll never defeat me,' she said, her jaw clenched.

Dialogue: -ing

'Of course, please help yourself,' the shopkeeper said, pointing at the magical potions on the shelf.

We can use a special form of a verb in our dialogue to show two things happening at once, or to be more precise about what is happening when the character is speaking. These '-ing' forms of the verb are called non-finite clauses (which is a fancy way of saying they aren't attached to a tense). You can't tell if it happened in the past, present or future. This means you have to have a verb (finite verb) that tells you when it happened in the same sentence.

Don't get too worried or bogged down with the grammar! Just remember, you can't use an -ing verb without a normal verb in the sentence.

For example, a sentence like this: *Running into the room, Gautum.* See how strange it sounds? We need to add a normal (finite) verb.

Running into the room, Gautum shouted for someone to help him.

Sentence structure

DIALOGUE + VERB + -ING VERB FORM (more information about the subject)

'__________,' + __________ + ____________________.

Examples

'Don't touch it,' the Wizard yelled, pointing a shaky finger at the crystal.

'Are you crazy? Don't touch it!' the magician shouted, throwing a velvet red cloth over his crystal ball.

Top tip

You can start the sentence with the -ing verb.

Pointing his shaky finger at the crystal, the Wizard yelled, 'Don't touch it.'

Dialogue versus feelings

> *'Don't worry, we will be fine,' said Michael, fighting back the rising panic surging through his body.*

I'm sure you can think of a time you told someone you were fine, but secretly you wanted to scream, collapse or cry (ask your class teacher about the last time they had an Ofsted visit). You can show internal conflict by having a character say one thing but contrasting it with their feelings or the feelings they are trying to overcome inside.

Sentence structure

DIALOGUE + WHO? + FEELING

________ + __________ + ___________.

Examples

'Of course it's no problem at all sir,' the waiter said, trying to hide the contempt in his face.

'I just need a minute,' Maddie said, her face glowing red with anger.

The sound of silence

'I'll miss you,' Sarah said. David didn't reply but stood in silence, staring at the floor.

Using silence is a simple trick to show how a character is feeling. We have all been in a conversation and realised that the other person is upset because they didn't respond. Using a character's silence to react can say more than a thousand words can.

Sentence structure

DIALOGUE – ADDING PAUSES + SILENCE FOR PHYSICAL REACTIONS

________________ + ________________________.

Top tip

Other reaction ideas for your writing:

Isaac paused.

Isaac fell into silence.

Isaac did not respond.

Hear my voice

'Get in the back of the van,' the policeman screamed, his voice like a wailing siren.

Giving your character a distinctive voice that reflects their true nature brings your dialogue to life. First, decide if it's a positive or negative feeling that you get when you hear your character speak. Then think of positive (lovely) and negative (horrible) sounds that you can compare the voice to. To compare the voice, we can use a simile (comparing one thing to another).

Sentence structure

DIALOGUE + WHO? + VOICE DESCRIPTION?

________________ + __________________ + ________________.

Examples

'Get out,' the woman screamed, her voice like fingernails scraping down a chalkboard.

'Come a little closer if you wish to see the gold,' said the dragon, its voice smooth as honey.

Changes in the voice

'Just get out of my room,' Charlotte said, her voice getting louder and louder.

Another writer's trick is to show a change in the character's feelings through a physical effect on their voice. To do this, we could change its volume, pitch or tone.

Sentence structure

DIALOGUE? + WHO? + VOLUME CHANGE?

'This is the ancient kingdom of the Polalis,' she said, her voice falling into a hushed whisper.

DIALOGUE? + WHO? + PITCH?

'You want me to go first? Into that dark tunnel?' Zafira protested, her voice becoming high-pitched and shrill.

DIALOGUE? + WHO? + TONE?

'I told you to drop the weapon,' the detective ordered, his voice becoming a low growl.

How to break up long sections of dialogue

'I knew this whole mission was flawed,' the captain muttered, folding her arms tight across her chest. 'I told you the coordinates were wrong.'

A simple trick for breaking up a long piece of dialogue is to place the subject in the middle and deliver it in two sections. This can be punctuated as either one longer sentence broken into two, or as two separate sentences.

Sentence structure

DIALOGUE + WHO? + WHAT? + DIALOGUE

__________ + WHO? + WHAT? + _____________.

Example

'You look scared,' Zafira observed, stepping closer to the wizard, who was fidgeting with his robes. 'But you're not scared of the crystal. You're scared of what happens when I actually manage to use it.'

Now where?

Well done for finishing your story! I hope you found the sentence models in this book helpful in getting you started with your writing. So, what now? Well, there are thousands of different sentences that you can use and an infinite number of ways of arranging them. If you want to move beyond using the sentence models in this book, then this is how to do it.

Keep a writing journal

Grab yourself a notebook and a pen. It doesn't have to be anything fancy. Just somewhere that is easy to access when you are reading. Now, the next time you are reading a book and you spot a sentence model you like, you can make a note of it in your book. Copy the sentence down. See what it is describing.

- A setting?
- A character?
- Look at the pattern.

Draw it out if you'd like, using a visual model, such as _____, _____ and _____.

Spend some time playing around with it. Even if the author has used the sentence pattern to describe a setting, you may be able to change it to describe a character's thoughts or actions.

Now, the next time you come to write a story, you will have your own sentence models book, packed full of fantastic ideas to use.

Pay attention to dialogue

If you start following people around with a notebook, writing down what they say, you are going to get some very strange looks (or the police will call you in!). Instead, if you want to see how great dialogue works, you need to take a look at your book collection. Grab one of your favourite books and skip through to find a dialogue section.

Annoyingly, nearly every book you come across has its own style and formatting of dialogue, but what you can look at is **how** the writer has used dialogue.

Pay attention to:

- What is being said?
- What is **not** being said? (Like pointless introductions or conversations about cornflakes.)

Are the characters talking about their goals (what they are trying to do in the story)?

Where does the dialogue reveal the plot or the story, so the writer doesn't have to directly? Do the characters have their own ways of speaking? What do we learn from the characters in what they are saying?

Notice the story shapes

Did you know that the same stories are just being told again and again? In fact, some experts say that there are only seven stories and that, although the settings and characters may change, the basic shape remains the same.

You probably recognise some of these story ideas:

- **Overcoming the monster**: A hero must face a scary 'bad guy' or a big problem (like a dragon or a bully) to save their home.
- **The quest**: A character goes on a long journey to find a specific object or reach a special place (like finding a hidden treasure).
- **Journey and return**: Someone travels to a strange, magical world (such as Wonderland or space) and eventually returns home with new wisdom.

Take a look at some of your favourite stories (these could also be from film or TV). Do you recognise this story being used?

Once you start recognising the story ideas (or story shapes), it makes it a lot easier for you to plan and write your own stories, as the truth is that all good authors copy each other and build on others' great ideas!